To:_____

From:_____

Date:_____

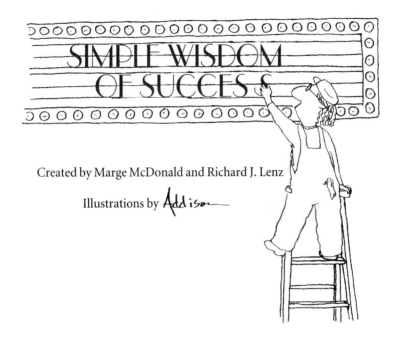

SIMPLE WISDOM OF SUCCESS

Created by Marge McDonald and Richard J. Lenz

Illustrations by Addison

Longstreet
Atlanta, Georgia

Published by LONGSTREET PRESS, INC.
A subsidiary of Cox Newspapers
A division of Cox Enterprises, Inc.
2140 Newmarket Parkway, Suite 122
Atlanta, Georgia 30309

Copyright © 1999 by McDonald & Lenz, Inc.
Design by Lenz Design & Communications, Inc., Decatur, GA

Printed in the United States of America, 1st printing, 1999.

Library of Congress Card Catalog Number: 98-89172
ISBN: 1-56352-541-0

*In many cases we've taken a little liberty with poets' and writers' lines to fit this book
but credited them where we knew who wrote the basic words. We sincerely hope
in their wisdom they forgive us.*

Quotations contribute something to the stability or enlargement of the language.
—*Samuel Johnson*

Always

acknowledge a mistake quite frankly. This will throw those in authority off their guard and give you an opportunity to commit more.

—*Mark Twain*

Ability is commonly found to consist mainly
in a big degree of solemnity.
—*Ambrose Bierce*

Aspire not, my soul, the life of the immortals,
but enjoy to the fullest that within thy reach.
—*Pindar*

Accept blame for your failures and give credit
where credit is due for your successes.
—*Proverbs*

Ability is nothing without opportunity.
You can create your own opportunity.
—*Napoleon Bonaparte*

Ah, but a man's reach *should* exceed his grasp, or what's a heaven for?
—*Robert Browning*

Appearance of being able makes you equal to the task.
—*Seneca*

A disciplined conscience is a man's best friend.
It may not be his most amiable,
but it is his most faithful monitor.
—*Henry Ward Beecher*

Anyone can hold the helm when the sea is calm.
—*Publilus Syrus*

An idea must be vigorous and positive, and without loose ends, so that it may
fulfill its divine mission and be productive.
—*Johann von Goethe*

Ambition has little rest.
—*Edward Bulwer-Lytton*

An ounce of loyalty is worth a pound of cleverness.
—*Elbert Hubbard*

An intelligent person aims at wise action,
but a fool starts off in many directions.
—*Proverbs*

Bureaucracy

FORM LINE
HERE
TO FIND OUT
WHAT LINE
YOU SHOULD
BE WAITING
IN

is the death
of any
achievement.
—*Albert Einstein*

Better honor than shameful wealth.
—*Eustache Deschamps*

Being critical is so much easier
than being correct.
—*Benjamin Disraeli*

Beware that you don't lose the substance
by grasping at the shadow.
—*Aesop*

Brevity is best, whether we are,
or are not, understood.
—*Samuel Butler*

Be satisfied with success in the smallest matter,
and know that even such a result is no trifle.
—*Marcus Aurelius Antoninus*

Be content for you cannot be first in all things.
—*Aesop*

Blessed are they who have nothing to say,
and who cannot
be persuaded to say it.
—*James Russell Lowell*

Better to be wise by the misfortunes of others
than by your own.
—*Aesop*

By trying the untried and not always
following instructions,
new discoveries are made.
—*Marcus Aurelius Antoninus*

Believe the one who has proved it.
Believe only an expert.
—*Virgil*

Between wavering capability
and indubitable performance
there's an ocean of difference.
—*Thomas Carlyle*

Confucius says:

To know that we know
what we know,
and that we do not know
what we do not know,
that is true knowledge.

Count no mistakes,
have no experience,
expect no wisdom.
—*Chinese saying*

Chance favors
the prepared mind.
—*Louis Pasteur*

Character is higher than intellect.
—*Ralph Waldo Emerson*

Credit goes to the person
who convinces the world,
not to the one to whom
the idea first occurs.
—*Sir William Osler*

Climbing steep hills
requires a slow pace
at first.
—*William Shakespeare*

Curiosity is one of
the certain characteristics
of a vigorous mind.
—*Samuel Johnston*

Certainly everyone has a right
to be conceited
but only until they are successful.
—*Benjamin Franklin*

Change and update your plans regularly
never losing sight
of your original goal.
—*Anonymous*

Command wisely and
you will be obeyed cheerfully.
—*Thomas Fuller*

Chance has nothing to do with that
that has not been prepared in advance.
—*Alexis de Tocqueville*

Don't

wait too long
for your ship
to come in,
the dock
might collapse.

—*Anonymous*

Do not try to manage too many jobs.
Like pumpkins in water, one pops up
while you try to hold down the other.
—*Chinese Proverb*

Determination and hard work conquer
most obstacles on the way to success.
—*Proverbs*

Delay is preferable to error.
—*Thomas Jefferson*

Defer not until tomorrow to be wise.
—*William Congreve*

Determined workers are able
because they think they are able.
—*Virgil*

Don't overload gratitude; if you do she'll kick.
—*Benjamin Franklin*

Don't mix business with pleasure,
the trouble is that th' pleasure allus
comes t' the top.
—*Abe Martin*

Definitely unfair, that's the law of work—
and there it is and nothing can change it:
The higher the pay in enjoyment
a man gets out of it,
the higher will be his pay in money also.
—*Mark Twain*

Difficulties exist to be surmounted.
—*Ralph Waldo Emerson*

Destiny is something that is achieved,
not given.
—*Proverbs*

Don't try to lead until you learn how—
then move as fast as possible.
—*Napoleon Bonaparte*

Even

when you're
on the right track,
you'll get run over
if you just sit there.
—*Will Rogers*

Enthusiasm is the best a person has to offer.
Even more than power or money.
—*Anonymous*

Even when you are aspiring to the highest place,
it is honorable to reach the second or
even the third rank.
—*Cicero*

Everything might be well,
if there was no *but* added to it.
—*German proverb*

Experience is the name
everyone gives
to his mistakes.
—*Oscar Wilde*

Even Noah got no salary for the first six months—
partly on account of the weather
and partly because he was learning navigation.
—*Mark Twain*

Experience that we do not call education
is more precious than that which we call so.
—*Ralph Waldo Emerson*

Each person must examine his own conduct.
If it is something to boast about, without having to compare it with
what someone else has done, it will at least be something of his own,
not just something better than his friends.
—*Galatians*

Experience is not what happens to a person,
it is that person does with what happens to them.
—*Aldous Leonard Huxley*

Each man's labor brings its own return.
—*German saying*

Education has at least one valuable lesson,
to make you do the thing you have to do,
when it ought to be done,
whether you like it or not.
—*Thomas Huxley*

Fear of failure
will be your fuel
to success.
—*Jewish saying*

For a thing to remain undone,
nothing more is required
than to think it done.
—*Baltasar Gracian*

Find two people in a business agreeing
and one of them
is unnecessary.
—*Anonymous*

Fortune smiles
and I smile to think,
how quickly she can frown.
—*Robert Southwell*

Fortune favors the bold.
—*Virgil*

Fame comes only when deserved,
and then is as inevitable as destiny,
for it is destiny.
—*Henry Wadsworth Longfellow*

For he that once is good,
is ever great!
—*Ben Jonson*

Far away in the sunshine
are my highest inspirations.
I may not reach them, but I can see the beauty,
believe in them, and try to follow where they may lead.
—*Louisa May Alcott*

Far and away the best prize
that life offers is the chance
to work hard
at work worth doing.
—*Theodore Roosevelt*

From fortune to misfortune is but a step;
from misfortune to fortune is a long way.
—*Yiddish saying*

Fame due to the achievements of the mind never perishes.
—*Propertius*

Genius

may have
its limitations,
but stupidity
is not thus
handicapped.
—*Elbert Hubbard*

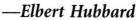

Give me a fruitful error any time, full of seeds,
bursting with its own corrections.
—*Vilfredo Pareto*

Get Place and Wealth; if possible with grace;
if not, by any means get Wealth and Place.
—*Alexander Pope*

Great men are those who do not lose their child's heart.
—*Mencius*

Get good advice and you will succeed;
don't go charging into battle without a plan.
—*Proverbs*

Great works are performed only by perseverance.
—*Samuel Johnson*

Genius is one percent inspiration
and ninety-nine percent perspiration.
—*Thomas Edison*

Goin' t' work will be found twice
as profitable as knockin' th' rich.
—*Abe Martin*

Great men owe most of their greatness
to the ability of detecting in those
from whom they learn their trade,
the exact quality that matters in their work.
—*Joseph Conrad*

Give your avocation
the same amount of time, attention,
and energy, as your vocation.
—*Anonymous*

Good people make thoughtful decisions;
the dishonest have to pretend as best they can.
—*Proverbs*

Great discoveries are made
only by exercising the imagination.
—*Anonymous*

He knew the precise psychological moment when to say nothing.
—*Oscar Wilde*

Happy the man who can search out
the causes of things.
—*Virgil*

He who heeds not experience,
trust him not.
—*John Boyle O'Reilly*

He has achieved success
who has lived well,
laughed often, and loved much.
—*Bessie Anderson Stanley*

He who strives to be rich in a day,
will be destroyed in a year.
—*Leonardo Da Vinci*

Hard work not only tends to give us
rest for the body,
but, what is even more important,
peace to the mind.
—*Sir John Lubbock*

Hard work always yields profit,
idle talk brings only want.
—*Proverbs*

Human improvement
is from within outwards.
—*James Froude*

He who neglects learning in his youth
loses the past and has no future.
—*Euripedes*

He has carried every point,
who has mingled the useful
with the agreeable.
—*Horace*

He who comes up to his own idea of greatness,
must always have had
a very low standard
of it in his mind.
—*William Hazlitt*

It's a terrible thing
to look over your shoulder
when you are trying to lead
and find no one there.
—*Franklin D. Roosevelt*

It is not enough to have a good mind.
The main thing is to use it well.
—*Rene Descartes*

I not only use the brains I have,
but all that I can borrow.
—*Woodrow Wilson*

It's what a feller thinks he knows that hurts him.
—*Abe Martin*

If you'd be wealthy,
think of giving more than getting.
—*Benjamin Franklin*

Intelligent people think before they speak;
what they say is then more persuasive.
—*Proverbs*

If you don't say anything, you won't be called upon to repeat it.
—*Calvin Coolidge*

It is sometimes expedient to forget who we are,
and we may with advantage at times forget
what we know.
—*Publilius Syrus*

If you pay attention when you are corrected,
you are wise.
—*Proverbs*

It is wonderful how much can be done
if we are always doing.
—*Thomas Jefferson*

In the area of human life
the honors and rewards
fall to those who show their good qualities in action.
—*Aristotle*

If I have been able to see farther than others,
it is because I stood
on the shoulders of giants.
—*Isaac Newton*

If passion drives,
let reason
hold the reins.
—*Benjamin Franklin*

I care not what others think
of what I do,
but I care very much
about what I think of what I do.
—*Theodore Roosevelt*

If you wish to reach the highest,
begin at the lowest.
—*Publilius Syrus*

In order that people
may be happy in their work,
three things are required:
they must be fit for it;
they must not overdo it,
and they must have a sense
of success in it.
—*John Ruskin*

It's very well to be thrifty,
but don't amass
a hoard of regrets.
—*Charles D'Orleans*

Industry pays debts,
despair increases them.
—*Benjamin Franklin*

It's a mighty fine thing t' know
when not t' know too much.
—*Abe Martin*

It takes time to bring excellence to maturity.
It does not matter
what you are thought to be,
but what you are.
—*Publilius Syrus*

Imagination imitates.
The critical spirit creates.
—*Oscar Wilde*

Just as one door closes
another door opens;
but we often look so long
and so regretfully
upon the closed door
that we do not see
the ones which open for us.
—*Alexander Graham Bell*

Keep

well clear
of the fool;
you will not find
wise lips there.
—*Proverbs*

Last

words are
for fools
who think
they haven't
said enough.
—*Karl Marx*

Let us be grateful
to Adam our benefactor.
He cut us out of
the "blessing" of idleness
and won for us
the "curse" of labor.
—*Mark Twain*

Look with favor upon a bold beginning.
—*Virgil*

Let all things be done
in a proper and orderly fashion.
—*Corinthians*

Listen and ye shall learn.
—*Latin proverb*

Let each man pass his days
in that wherein
his skill is greatest.
—*Propertius*

Let us be thankful for the fools;
but for them the rest of us could not succeed.
—*Mark Twain*

Leaders do not lead by hitting people
over the head—that's assault, not leadership.
—*Dwight D. Eisenhower*

Live today by what we know to be right today,
and be ready tomorrow to call it false.
—*William James*

Let reason prevail with you more than popular opinion.
—*Cicero*

Live and Think!
—*Samuel Lover*

Let others hail the rising sun;
bow only to those whose course is run.
—*David Garrick*

Make

sure you don't
end up the richest person
in the cemetery.
You can't do business
from there.
—*Colonel Sanders*

My heart bids me to do it if I can,
and my head if it is
a thing possible to do.
—*Homer*

Money is like manure.
It's not worth anything
unless it is spread around
to make things grow!
—*Anonymous*

Maneuver your failures
into lessons for success.
—*German proverb*

Most people will succeed in small things
if they were not troubled
with great ambitions.
—*Henry Wadsworth Longfellow*

Mistakes bring wisdom.
—*Spanish saying*

Making a few failures early in life
is of the greatest practical benefit.
—*Thomas Huxley*

Most o' th' studyin'
is done out o' college.
—*Abe Martin*

Man's worth is no greater
than the worth of his ambitions.
—*Marcus Aurelius*

Make it a point to do something
every day that you don't want to do.
This is the golden rule
for acquiring the habit
of doing your duty without pain.
—*Mark Twain*

Man needs a certain amount
of intelligent ignorance to succeed.
—*French saying*

Never
substitute
your identity
with the envy
of another.
—*Proverbs*

Nothin' is as uncommon as common sense.
—*Abe Martin*

Never over promise what you can do,
but always render more than you promised.
—*Proverbs*

Nothing is so firmly believed as what we least know.
—*Michael de Montaigne*

No estimate is more in danger of erroneous calculations
than those by which a man computes
the force of his own genius.
—*Samuel Johnson*

Never say more than is necessary.
—*Richard Brinsley Sheridan*

Nothing is impossible for the person
who doesn't have to do it himself.
—*Anonymous*

No man is really happy or successful without a hobby—
anything will do so long as he straddles
the hobby and rides it hard.
—*Sir William Osler*

No circumstances can repair a defect of character.
—*Ralph Waldo Emerson*

Next to doing the right thing, it is important
to let people know you are doing the right thing.
—*John D. Rockefeller*

No one can direct when all pretend to know.
—*Oliver Goldsmith*

Never sleep 'till nine a.m.
The feller that does might as well stay in bed.
—*Abe Martin*

Never are those who have bent themselves
able to make others straight.
—*Menciuse*

Out of intense complexities intense simplicities will emerge.
—*Winston Churchill*

Our greatest mistake is to imagine
that we never err.
—*Thomas Carlyle*

Out of every success comes something
to make a new effort necessary.
—*Walt Whitman*

One machine can do the work of fifty men.
No machine can do the work
of one extraordinary man.
—*Elbert Hubbard*

Our thoughts and our conduct are our own.
—*James Froude*

Only the mediocre are always at their best.
—*Yiddish proverb*

Our aspirations are our possibilities.
—*Robert Browning*

One person's failure
can well be another's success.
Measure yours carefully.
—*Anonymous*

One is silent when we disrust our own choices
or think we are unwise.
—*French saying*

One of the greatest pains
to human nature
is the pain of a new idea.
—*Walter Bagehot*

Our judgment is gained with years,
or else years are in vain.
—*Owen Meredith*

Of nothing you can,
in the long-run
and with much lost labour,
make only—Nothing.
—*Thomas Carlyle*

The
Principal
mark of genius
is not perfection
but originality.
—*Plato*

Perseverance is a great element of success.
—*Henry Wadsworth Longsfellow*

Put your money in trust, not your trust in money.
—*Oliver Wendell Holmes*

Perseverance, n. A virtue whereby mediocrity
achieves a glorious success.
—*Ambrose Bierce*

Plan with audacity—execute with vigor.
—*Anonymous*

People who cannot find time for recreation
are obliged sooner or later to find time for illness.
—*John Wanamaker*

Power of accurate observation
is commonly called cynicism
by those who have not got it.
—*George Bernard Shaw*

Progress is the mother of problems,
but mostly those that can be solved.
—*G. K. Chesterton*

Pray to God for a good harvest,
but don't stop hoeing.
—*Bohemian proverb*

Praise for a job well done motivates.
—*Anonymous*

Polished idleness brings forth frivolous work.
—*Sir James Mackintosh*

A person who occupies the first place
seldom plays the principal part.
—*Johann von Goethe*

Power is more safely retained by caution
than by severe actions.
—*Tacitus*

Quite
right that
those that shared
in the labor
should share
in the honors.

Rewards

**in business go to
the person who
has ideas
and the energy
to make them work.**

—Anonymous

Sometimes

it is as hard
to tell the truth
as to hide it.

—*Baltasar Gracian*

Success for the striver washes away
the demands of striving.
—*Roman Saying*

Success carries a strong sense of obligation.
—*Jewish proverb*

Speak the loudest
and you'll be the least heard.
—*Anonymous*

Success follows the bold
and slights the fainthearted.
—*Ralph Waldo Emerson*

Success is achieved for three reasons:
ability, courage, and luck!
—*Anonymous*

Self-trust is the first secret of success.
—*Ralph Waldo Emerson*

Seek good advice and you will succeed;
never enter a battle
without a plan.
—*Julius Caeser*

Successful folks are the ones
who dream up things
for the rest of the world to keep busy at.
—*Mark Twain*

Small successes suffice
for small souls.
—*Nestell Boyee*

See everything;
overlook a great deal;
correct when needed.
—*Roman saying*

Silence of pure innocence,
persuades where speaking fails.
—*William Shakespeare*

Those born
with a talent which
is meant to be used
find their greatest joy
in using it.
—*Johann von Goethe*

The world is moving so fast these days
that the man who says it can't be done
is often interrupted
by someone doing it.
—*Elbert Hubbard*

Talent without genius is something;
but genius without talent is nothing.
—*Alexis de Tocqueville*

Those least dependent on tomorrow
go to meet it with the greater enthusiasm.
—*Epicurus*

To succeed we do everything we can
to appear successful.
—*Francois Duc de La Rochefoucauld*

The path to success can be elusive
but the sure path to failure
is to try to please everyone.
—*Anonymous*

There is only one success—to be able to spend
your life in your own way.
—*Christopher Morley*

The secret to reaching my goals
lies solely in my tenacity.
—*Louis Pasteur*

The secret of success is constancy to purpose.
—*Benjamin Disraeli*

There is no need to parade your gifts of mind, others will find them.
—*Proverbs*

Trust your own judgment,
for it is your most reliable counselor.
—*Ecclesiastes*

The noblest spirit is most strongly attracted
by the love of glory.
—*Cicero*

The direction in which education starts
you will determine your future life.
—*Plato*

To have an uncluttered mind at the end of each day,
make a list of everything,
even the little things,
that you must accomplish the next day.
Then, make sure you end that day
with a clean slate.
—*Benjamin Franklin*

There is nothing so constant in this world as change.
—*Jonathan Swift*

There is no sin except stupidity.
—*Oscar Wilde*

There are no grades of vanity,
there are only grades of ability
in concealing it.
—*Mark Twain*

To do two things at once is to do neither well.
Amid a multitude of projects,
no plan devised.
—*Pulilius Syrus*

There is no kind of idleness
by which we are so easily seduced
as that which dignifies itself
by the appearance of work.
—*Samuel Johnson*

The successful take risks!
—*Benjamin Franklin*

There is great skill in knowing when
to conceal one's skill.
—*Francois Duc de La Rochefoucauld*

The secret of success is to be ready
for opportunity
when it comes.
—*Benjamin Disraeli*

Unless you know where you're going, all roads will lead to nowhere.

—*Anonymous*

NO PLACE

NULLTOWN

LOSTROPOLIS

VACANTBURG

VOIDSVILLE

Vision
is the talent
to see things
invisible.
—Jonathan Swift

When

your work
speaks for itself
don't interpret.
—*Proverbs*

When complimented before others
simply offer a simpler thank-you.
—*Proverbs*

Who does the best circumstances allow,
does well, acts nobly;
angels could do no more.
—*Charles Young*

Wisdom outweighs wealth.
—*Sophocles*

Wishing is of little account;
to succeed you must earnestly desire;
and this desire
must shorten your sleep.
—*Ovid*

We have not the love of greatness,
but the love of the love
of greatness.
—*Thomas Carlyle*

Well-expressed ideas are like a design of gold, set in silver.
—*Proverbs*

What you cannot enforce, do not demand.
—*Sophocles*

What impresses is not the mind
but the energy and enthusiasm.
—*Walter Bagehot*

When they come down from their Ivory Towers,
idealists are apt to walk straight into the gutter.
—*Logan Pearsall Smith*

When you are happy
you will know success.
—*Abe Martin*

When we shall have succeeded,
then will be our time to rejoice, and freely laugh.
—*Theodore Buckely*

You can't
eXpect
to win unless
you know
why you lose.
—*Benjamin Franklin*

You can't
build a reputation
on what you are
planning to do.
—*Henry Ford*

Zeal makes more
men's fortunes
than cautiousness.
—*Marquis de Vauvenargues*

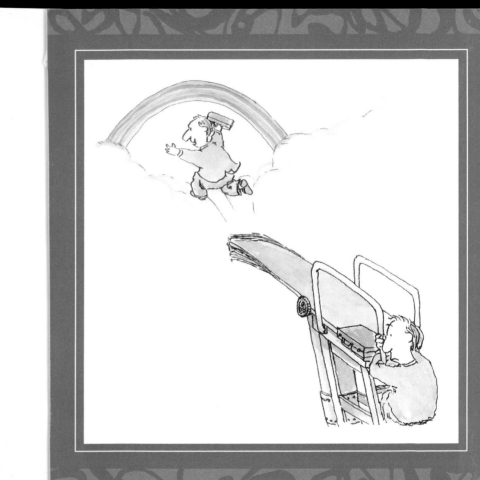

The race by vigour,
not by vaunts is won.
—*Alexander Pope*

The race by vigour,
not by vaunts is won.
—*Alexander Pope*